Spring Harvest
Bible Workbook

JOHN

Jesus at the centre

Jenny Baker

Series editor for thematic workbooks – Jeff Lucas

Authentic

MILTON KEYNES • COLORADO SPRINGS • HYDERABAD

SPRING
HARVEST

Equipping the Church for action

Copyright © 2001 Jenny Baker

14 13 12 11 10 09 08   10 9 8 7 6 5 4

Reprinted in 2004, 2007, 2008 by Spring Harvest Publishing Division and Authentic Media
Authentic Media, 9 Holdom Avenue, Bletchley, Milton Keynes, Bucks., MK1 1QR
1820 Jet Stream Drive, Colorado Springs, CO 80921, USA
OM Authentic Media, Medchal Road, Jeedimetla Village, Secunderabad 500 055, A.P., India

www.authenticmedia.co.uk

Authentic Media is a division of IBS-STL U.K., limited by guarantee, with its Registered
Office at Kingstown Broadway, Carlisle, Cumbria CA3 0HA. Registered in England &
Wales No. 1216232. Registered charity 270162

British Library Cataloguing in Publication Data

A catalogue record for this book is available from the British Library

ISBN 978-1-85078-440-1

Typeset by Spring Harvest
Printed and bound in Great Britain by J.H. Haynes & Co., Sparkford
Print management by Adare Carwin

CONTENTS

ABOUT THIS BOOK

This study book aims to help you consider how to put Jesus at the centre of your life, in all you do and all you think. It is based on passages in John, but doesn't attempt to cover the whole gospel.

This workbook is written primarily for use in a group situation, but can easily be used by individuals who want to study the biblical picture of God. It can be used in a variety of contexts, so it is perhaps helpful to spell out the assumptions that we have made about the groups that will use it. These can have a variety of names – home groups, Bible study groups, cell groups – we've used housegroup as the generic term.

▶ The emphasis of the studies will be on the application of the Bible. Group members will not just learn facts, but will be encouraged to think: 'How does this apply to me? What change does it require of me? What incidents or situations in my life is this relevant to?'

▶ Housegroups can encourage honesty and make space for questions and doubts. The aim of the studies is not to find the 'right answer', but to help members understand the Bible by working through the questions. The Christian faith throws up paradoxes. Events in people's lives may make particular verses difficult to understand. The housegroup should be a safe place to express these concerns.

▶ Housegroups can give opportunities for deep friendships to develop. Group members will be encouraged to talk about their experiences, feelings, questions, hopes and fears. They will be able to offer one another pastoral support and to get involved in each other's lives.

▶ There is a difference between being a collection of individuals who happen to meet together every Wednesday and being an effective group who bounce ideas off each other, spark inspiration and creativity and pool their talents and resources to create solutions together and whose whole is definitely greater than the sum of its parts. The process of working through these studies will encourage healthy group dynamics.

Space is given for you to write answers, comments, questions and thoughts. This book will not tell you what to think, but will help you to discover the truth of God's word through thinking, discussing, praying and listening.

FOR GROUP MEMBERS

▶ You will get more out of the study if you spend some time during the week reading the passage and thinking about the questions. Make a note of anything you don't understand.

▶ Pray that God will help you to understand the passage and show you how to apply it. Pray for other members in the group too, that they will find the study helpful.

▶ Be willing to take part in the discussions. The leader of the group is not there as an expert with all the answers. They will want everyone to get involved and share their thoughts and opinions.

▶ However, don't dominate the group! If you are aware that you are saying a lot, make space for others to contribute. Be sensitive to other group members and aim to be encouraging. If you disagree with someone, say so but without putting down their contribution.

FOR INDIVIDUALS

▶ Although this book is written with a group in mind, it can also be easily used by individuals. You obviously won't be able to do the group activities suggested, but you can consider how you would answer the questions and write your thoughts in the space provided.

▶ You may find it helpful to talk to a prayer partner about what you have learnt, and ask them to pray for you as you try and apply what you are learning to your life.

▶ The New International Version of the text is printed in the book. If you usually use a different version, then read from your own Bible as well.

INTRODUCTION

In our busy, multicultural, postmodern society where Jesus increasingly seems to be pushed to the edges, we are going to dare to ask 'What would happen if we put Jesus at the centre of everything we do and everything we think?'

The word Christian appears three times in the New Testament; the word disciple appears nearly three hundred times. As followers of Jesus, if we are to be true to his calling, we need to be people who continue to grow and learn throughout our lives. Not content just to call ourselves Christians, we want to be people whose lives demonstrate the love and power of Jesus in a way that cannot be ignored by those outside the church.

We need to know who Jesus is and what he was like – we will look at his humanity and the life he shared with his disciples. We need to know what kind of life he calls us to lead – we will examine the banquet as a metaphor for the rich, unhurried life Jesus offers us. We need to learn how to relate to each other properly in a broken and fallen world – we will look at Jesus' relationships with his Father, his friends and the world around him and discover how we can model ourselves on him.

These studies are based on the gospel of John, drawing mainly from Jesus' words to the disciples in the upper room as they shared the last Passover meal together. As Jesus approached the cross, he prepared his disciples for their coming mission and the part they would play in the life of the early church. Anointed by the Holy Spirit, those words provided a powerful foundation for people who would call so many to follow their Lord Jesus. What better place for us to start as we consider life with Jesus at the centre?

LEARNING FROM
THE HUMANITY OF JESUS

AIM: To investigate the humanity of Jesus and its relevance to our lives

In the beginning was the Word, and the Word was with God, and the Word was God. He was with God in the beginning.

Through him all things were made; without him nothing was made that has been made. In him was life, and that life was the light of men. The light shines in the darkness, but the darkness has not understood it.

There came a man who was sent from God; his name was John. He came as a witness to testify concerning that light, so that through him all men might believe. He himself was not the light; he came only as a witness to the light. The true light that gives light to every man was coming into the world.

He was in the world, and though the world was made through him, the world did not recognise him. He came to that which was his own, but his own did not receive him. Yet to all who received him, to those who believed in his name, he gave the right to become children of God—children born not of natural descent, nor of human decision or a husband's will, but born of God.

The Word became flesh and made his dwelling among us. We have seen his glory, the glory of the One and Only, who came from the Father, full of grace and truth.

John 1:1–14

TO SET THE SCENE

Bring photos to this session of yourself when you were younger. You could bring a photo from each decade of your lives, or find two or three key moments or memories that you would like others to know about. These photos show your history, your growing up. Jesus would not have had a camera but he too had memories from when he was a child, or a teenager or a young adult.

READ JOHN 1:1-14

WHAT DOES
SEARCH
THE BIBLE SAY?
1. John wrote his gospel so that 'you may believe that Jesus is the Christ, the Son of God, and that by believing you may have life in his name.' John 20:31. What statements in this passage point to Jesus' divinity, the fact that he was fully God?

2. And yet Jesus was also fully human (v14). *The Message* expresses this verse in this way: 'The Word became flesh and blood and moved into the neighbourhood.' Make a list of activities that Jesus did that demonstrate his humanity. Add emotions and feelings that Jesus showed and experienced while he was here on earth.

3. Jesus was both human and God – a difficult concept for us to grasp. What happens if we emphasise his divinity more than his humanity? And what happens if we highlight his humanity and forget that he was also God? What stops us appreciating the humanity of Jesus?

4. Look at the creed on Page 11. Which lines sum up the life of Jesus? The important facts are there but a lot of the detail is missing! Write some sentences of belief that affirm the reality of Jesus' humanity.

> *'The Creed hustles through Jesus' life in one paragraph, beginning with his birth and skipping immediately to his death, descent into hell and ascent into heaven. Wait a minute – isn't something missing? What happened in the interval between his being born of the Virgin Mary and his suffering under Pontius Pilate? Somehow everything Jesus said and did in thirty-three years on earth gets swept aside in the rush to interpret his life. How did he spend his time here?'*
>
> **Philip Yancey**

HOW DOES THIS
APPLY TO ME
5. What difference does Jesus' life make to us? Firstly he is our life example. Jesus said to his disciples 'follow me.' This meant physically going with him, but they also learnt to imitate him, to model themselves on him.

Jesus says the same to us. What actions of Jesus do you find it most difficult to imitate?

6. It has been said that the church would rather worship Jesus than follow him. Do you agree?

7. Secondly, Jesus is our life source. Read John 15:1–5, where Jesus describes himself as the vine – 'apart from me you can do nothing.' Does this contradict the need to imitate Jesus? How much depends on our effort, and how much his enabling?

8. Thirdly, Jesus is our life lens – the one through whom we should view every part of life. Pick an area of life, and discuss how a Christ-centred approach to that area will make a difference.

9. Think about the kind of lifestyle often portrayed in adverts. What kind of life does the world entice us to live? How is the life of a follower of Jesus to be different – in lifestyle and in motivation?

> *'You and I are called to be persons after the manner of Jesus. Nothing else matters. Our goal is to become as Christ, to always have his image before our eyes.'*
>
> **Brennan Manning**

One image of the life that Jesus calls us to is that of a banquet – a long, carefully prepared celebration of relationships where people linger in conversation, deepening friendships, being nourished physically, emotionally and spiritually. Jesus doesn't come as the fast food distributor of blessings. Rather he invites us to live a life in his company, a life centred on the one who blesses and not just his blessing. Next week you will enjoy a meal together as you explore this in more depth!

WORSHIP

Read the Nicene Creed together. Pause after 'and was made man' and give space for people to read out their statements of belief about the humanity of Jesus. Then read the rest of the creed. Follow this with a time of prayer, thanking Jesus for entering into our world.

DURING THE WEEK

Many Christian young people wear bracelets with WWJD on to remind them to ask What Would Jesus Do? in everyday situations. Think of a way that you can remind yourself during the week to stop every so often, and remember that Jesus did the first century equivalent of whatever activity you are doing at the time − travelling to work, being entertained, bathing, eating and so on. Set your watch to bleep on the hour, or wear a ring on a different finger, or keep a small stone in your pocket − anything that will be a subtle reminder to think differently.

FOR FURTHER STUDY

Look through John and find the statements that John makes about Jesus and life. Which refer to eternal life in the future, and which to life now? What can you discover about the difference that Jesus makes to life here on earth now?

Try these passages to start with:
John 1:4; John 3:16; John 3:36; John 5:21; John 6:35; John 10:10; John 11:25; John 17:3; John 20:31.

In the synoptic gospels − Matthew, Mark and Luke − life is almost always viewed as being in the future. Paul and John both wrote about this future element of life, but resurrection life is also viewed as something that is to be enjoyed now by followers of Jesus.

THE NICENE CREED

We believe in one God, the Father, the Almighty,
maker of heaven and earth, of all that is, seen and unseen.

We believe in one Lord, Jesus Christ,
the only son of God,
eternally begotten of the Father,
God from God, Light from Light,
true God from true God,
begotten, not made,
of one being with the Father;
through him all things were made.
For us and for our salvation he came down from heaven;
by the power of the Holy Spirit he became incarnate of the Virgin Mary
and was made man.
For our sake he was crucified under Pontius Pilate;
he suffered death and was buried.
On the third day he rose again
in accordance with the Scriptures;
he ascended into heaven
and is seated at the right hand of the Father.
He will come again in glory to judge the living and the dead,
and his kingdom will have no end.

We believe in the Holy Spirit,
The Lord, the giver of life,
Who proceeds from the Father and the Son.
With the Father and the Son he is worshipped and glorified.
He has spoken through the prophets.

We believe in one holy catholic and apostolic church.
We acknowledge one baptism for the forgiveness of sins.
We look for the resurrection of the dead,
and the life of the world to come. Amen.

THE BANQUET – FOOD AND FRIENDSHIP

AIM: To learn from the 'banquet' as a metaphor for the Christian life

TO SET THE SCENE

Tonight is a night of food, conversation and friendship, with Jesus present as your guest. Why not start with a prayer, asking Jesus to be at the centre of your meal?

On the third day a wedding took place at Cana in Galilee. Jesus' mother was there, and Jesus and his disciples had also been invited to the wedding. When the wine was gone, Jesus' mother said to him, They have no more wine.

Dear woman, why do you involve me? Jesus replied. My time has not yet come.

His mother said to the servants, Do whatever he tells you.

Nearby stood six stone water jars, the kind used by the Jews for ceremonial washing, each holding from twenty to thirty gallons.

Jesus said to the servants, Fill the jars with water; so they filled them to the brim.

Then he told them, Now draw some out and take it to the master of the banquet.

They did so, and the master of the banquet tasted the water that had been turned into wine. He did not realise where it had come from, though the servants who had drawn the water knew. Then he called the bridegroom aside and said, Everyone brings out the choice wine first and then the cheaper wine after the guests have had too much to drink; but you have saved the best till now.

This, the first of his miraculous signs, Jesus performed at Cana in Galilee. He thus revealed his glory, and his disciples put their faith in him.

After this he went down to Capernaum with his mother and brothers and his disciples. There they stayed for a few days.

John 2:1–12

Before the starter
Read John 2:1–12

DISCUSS

1. This was the first miracle, or sign as John calls it, that Jesus did. Who would have seen it happen? What's your reaction to this miracle?

2. Jesus produced a better wine than the one the guests had already had. What does this say about the kingdom of God that Jesus came to bring in?

3. There would have been no water left for ceremonial washing. What was the significance of this?

To discuss as you eat the starter

4. Jesus was well known for eating and drinking (Matt11:19). Can you think of other stories from the gospels where he ate with people?

5. Share stories of how your Christian life has been a banquet experience – times of celebration, of deep friendships, of being nourished. How can we make our lives more banquet-like?

Before the main course
Read John 6:48–51

Jesus himself is part of the feast, the very bread of life. This is the first of his 'I am...' sayings.

To discuss as you eat the main course

6. What is the significance of Jesus calling himself bread as opposed to, say, chocolate gateau?

7. Bread needs to be eaten in order to sustain us. Share stories of ways in which you have been nourished or sustained by Jesus. How can we 'eat' more of Jesus?

Before dessert
Read Luke 14:1–24

Jesus teaches banquet protocol – how to behave and who is invited.

To discuss as you eat dessert

HOW DOES THIS **8.** What does this passage say about how to behave and who is included in the banquet life of being a follower of APPLY TO ME Christ? Share stories and ideas of how your housegroup, your church or any of the other communities you belong to – such as the workplace, neighbourhood, parents at the school gates, clubs – can include and make welcome those who feel, or are, uninvited and unwelcome.

WORSHIP
If it is appropriate, share communion together at the end of the meal.

Choose some words of liturgy to introduce the communion, or read Paul's words from 1 Corinthians 11:23–26.

A suggestion for prayer – have nightlights on the table and a central candle. As people pray for each other they can light a nightlight and leave it burning, a visual reminder of the prayers that have been prayed.

Read these words:

Jesus was a guest – of humanity
The heavenly host, who laid on a harvest of abundance for the world,
the creator, my provider, became a guest of the animals in the stable,
the villagers of Nazareth, the religious leaders in the Temple,
the prostitutes, drunkards, tax collectors.
He let us play host, did away with the VIP pass, ate, drank and was probably
merry.
Became one of us, dined at our table.
Ate the same bread, drank the same wine – everybody having a good time.
Shared stories; shared our story.

When he left the table, he left bread and wine.
He, himself, left; but he left himself.
The guest, once more, became the consummate host.

Words by Brian Draper
Reproduced by permission

DURING THE WEEK

Who do you invite to your house for meals? In Luke 14, Jesus says that we should invite round people who are unlikely to invite us back. Think about whether you would like to invite round for a meal people that you don't know very well, especially those who don't yet know Jesus. You need have no other agenda than to spend some time with them and to get to know them better.

FOR FURTHER STUDY

Talking about our lives as a Jesus-centred banquet doesn't mean that they will be untouched by pain or trouble – sometimes God sets a table for us 'in the presence of our enemies' (Psa 23:5). How would you encourage someone who is having a difficult time that the banquet picture is still appropriate to them? Have you had experiences where you were surprised by the presence and love of God in the midst of difficulty or despair?

BECOMING DISCIPLES OF CHRIST

AIM: To learn more about discipleship from Jesus' relationships with his disciples

The disciples spent three years with Jesus. They shared everyday activities such as eating and travelling, witnessed his miracles, heard his teaching and were trusted to be part of his ministry. We might be envious of that closeness, but what can we learn from Jesus' relationships with his disciples about the type of disciples we should be?

"I am the true vine, and my Father is the gardener. He cuts off every branch in me that bears no fruit, while every branch that does bear fruit he prunes so that it will be even more fruitful. You are already clean because of the word I have spoken to you. Remain in me, and I will remain in you. No branch can bear fruit by itself; it must remain in the vine. Neither can you bear fruit unless you remain in me.

"I am the vine; you are the branches. If a man remains in me and I in him, he will bear much fruit; apart from me you can do nothing. If anyone does not remain in me, he is like a branch that is thrown away and withers; such branches are picked up, thrown into the fire and burned. If you remain in me and my words remain in you, ask whatever you wish, and it will be given you. This is to my Father's glory, that you bear much fruit, showing yourselves to be my disciples.

"As the Father has loved me, so have I loved you. Now remain in my love. If you obey my commands, you will remain in my love, just as I have obeyed my Father's commands and remain in his love. I have told you this so that my joy may be in you and that your joy may be complete. My command is this: Love each other as I have loved you. Greater love has no one than this, that he lay down his life for his friends. You are my friends if you do what I command. I no longer call you servants, because a servant does not know his master's business. Instead, I have called you friends, for everything that I learned from my Father I have made known to you. You did not choose me, but I chose you and appointed you to go and bear fruit—fruit that will last. Then the Father will give you whatever you ask in my name. This is my command: Love each other."

John 15:1–17

TO SET THE SCENE

  Think back to your school days – was your school an effective place of learning? Can anyone remember things that they learned parrot-fashion but have never used – like Latin verbs or the periodic table? What experiences or people have you learned the most from in your life?

Read John 15:1-17

1. Look in John's gospel at what happens before and after Jesus says these words. What other things does he talk to the disciples about? What do you think was his intention in this section of teaching?

2. What does the word disciple mean? What is the difference between a convert and a disciple?

  3. What type of learning opportunities did Jesus give his disciples? Look at these passages for some ideas: John 2:11; Mat- thew 5:1–12, 10:1–15, 14:22–33, 18:1–6, 26:36–46; Luke 9:18–21. How can we have similar experiences today?

  4. Jesus describes how a branch bears fruit. First it is pruned. How does 'pruning' take place in our lives?

  5. Secondly it remains part of the vine. How do we do this (v10)? Which is more important in discipleship – our behaviour or our relationship with Jesus?

6. Why are we to bear fruit?

7. What difference does it make that Jesus has chosen us rather than us choosing Jesus?

'I am the true vine.' A vine was the symbol of Israel. When Jesus said that he was the true vine he was saying that, in contrast to Israel, he was the obedient son who would fulfil the calling of Israel, to be a light to the Gentiles (Isa 49:6).

To think about
Why do people grow vines?

Where does a vine end and the branches begin?

WORSHIP
On a large sheet of paper create a vine that represents your housegroup. Draw a trunk in the middle, then each person should draw a branch that represents themselves. Draw leaves on the branches and write on them words or symbols for the things you want to do in response to this session. You may need to take it in turns to draw!

Then pray for each other – use marker pens to draw bunches of grapes on someone's branch as you pray for them to be more fruitful.

DURING THE WEEK
A healthy and prayerful activity – decide to eat some fruit each day, and as you do so pray for one person in the group to be more fruitful as a disciple.

FOR FURTHER STUDY
Jesus says that if we obey his commands we will remain in his love (v10) and will be his friends (v14). What are the commands of Jesus? Start with this passage and list any commands that Jesus makes. Can you think of any others? How did Jesus sum up the law and the prophets (Matt 22:37)?

How can we stop ourselves falling into the trap of legalism – trying to gain salvation by keeping laws?

ACTIVITY PAGE

HOW FRUITY ARE YOU?
Look at the different types of fruit below – can you
think of recent examples of these in your life? Which
fruits do you think are least evident? Show this page
to someone who knows you and ask whether they
agree with you.

Introducing people to Jesus
– Luke 10:2

Justice
– Isaiah 5:7

Righteousness
– Isaiah 5:7

Mercy
– Micah 6:8

Love for one another
– John 13:35

**Love, joy, peace, patience, kindness, goodness,
faithfulness, gentleness, self-control**
– Galatians 5:22, 23

KNOWING GOD AND BEING KNOWN

AIM: to consider how we can provide the right conditions for our relationship with the Father to grow

"Do not let your hearts be troubled. Trust in God; trust also in me. In my Father's house are many rooms; if it were not so, I would have told you. I am going there to prepare a place for you. And if I go and prepare a place for you, I will come back and take you to be with me that you also may be where I am. You know the way to the place where I am going."

Thomas said to him, "Lord, we don't know where you are going, so how can we know the way?"

Jesus answered, "I am the way and the truth and the life. No one comes to the Father except through me. If you really knew me, you would know my Father as well. From now on, you do know him and have seen him."

Philip said, "Lord, show us the Father and that will be enough for us."

Jesus answered: "Don't you know me, Philip, even after I have been among you such a long time? Anyone who has seen me has seen the Father. How can you say, 'Show us the Father'? Don't you believe that I am in the Father, and that the Father is in me? The words I say to you are not just my own. Rather, it is the Father, living in me, who is doing his work. Believe me when I say that I am in the Father and the Father is in me; or at least believe on the evidence of the miracles themselves. I tell you the truth, anyone who has faith in me will do what I have been doing. He will do even greater things than these, because I am going to the Father. And I will do whatever you ask in my name, so that the Son may bring glory to the Father. You may ask me for anything in my name, and I will do it."

John 14:1–14

TO SET THE SCENE

Think about your friendships, especially those people that you have known for a long time or know very well. What were the key moments that cemented those friendships? Doing things together, rather than just talking, needing to find a solution to a problem together, or sharing the same concerns all help to cement friendships. Are there any parallels in our relationship with God?

Read John 14:1–14

1. In the gospel of John, Jesus talks about his relationship with his Father a lot. What does he say about it in this passage?

WHAT DOES SEARCH THE BIBLE SAY? **2.** Read these other verses from John. What do they tell you about Jesus' relationship with his Father? John 5:19, 6:57, 10:30, 13:1, 14:6, 14:21

WHAT DOES SEARCH THE BIBLE SAY? **3.** Maybe Jesus had a head start on us in knowing the Father, but he still made space for that relationship to grow. John expresses the depth of the relationship but we need to turn to Luke to see how the relationship was nurtured. What did Jesus do? Luke 6:12, 4:1,2, 5:16, 4:16

HOW DOES THIS APPLY TO ME **4.** If Jesus needed to provide the right conditions for his relationship with his Father to grow, how much more do we need to do so?! Throughout history people have practised spiritual disciplines as a means of getting closer to God. Look at the other disciplines listed on Page 22. Has anyone found any of these helpful? Are there other ways in which you have nurtured your relationship with God?

> *The disciplines place us before God; they do not give us Brownie points with God.*
>
> *Richard Foster*

We can't look at all of these in one session, but will examine a few. It is possible to misuse the disciplines – by thinking that they earn us favour with God, for example. We need to get beyond that and practise them to enjoy a richer relationship with our Father.

5. A new Christian asks you to give them some helpful hints on prayer. What practical guidelines and ideas can you offer?

HOW DOES THIS

APPLY TO ME

6. Quiet times – a time set aside each day for Bible study and prayer – seem to be less common than they once were. Do you have a regular time for prayer and study? What have you found helpful?

7. 'It must have been simple for people in the past to be quiet or go on retreat. It's just impossible and impractical in our busy lifestyles.' Do you agree? Where can you find silence and solitude in everyday life?

8. The church is perhaps not well known for celebration, although yours might be different. What would you think if your church cancelled a Sunday night service in order to have a big party? How can we celebrate more, corporately and individually?

Richard Foster's classic book Celebration of Discipline talks about these disciplines:

Inward disciplines
meditation, prayer, fasting, study

Outward disciplines
simplicity, solitude, submission, service

Corporate disciplines
confession, worship, guidance, celebration

There are also other disciplines that have been practised by Christians.

WORSHIP

Take a small plant pot, fill it with earth and plant a seed. On a label, write the disciplines that you want to develop in order to provide the right environment for your relationship with your Father to grow. Attach this to the pot. Pray for one another and take the pot home to look after.

DURING THE WEEK

Try a new routine for spiritual discipline this week. Although we can't expect to be transformed in one week, sometimes we need a new impetus to change our pattern of doing things. Identify two or three slots in the week when you could spend time in prayer, or study, or solitude, or a day or time when you can fast... Each of us needs to decide what suits us and our lifestyle best, but do accept the challenge to try something new!

FOR FURTHER STUDY

Read through the gospel of John and identify all the times that Jesus talks about his relationship with his Father. A concordance might be helpful.

What can you learn about Jesus' sense of calling? How did he know what to do? What can you discover about his identity, and how we are included in that relationship between Jesus and his Father?

CHURCH AND OUR RELATIONSHIPS

AIM: To examine the kinds of relationships that Jesus calls us to within the body of Christ

It was just before the Passover Feast. Jesus knew that the time had come for him to leave this world and go to the Father. Having loved his own who were in the world, he now showed them the full extent of his love.

The evening meal was being served, and the devil had already prompted Judas Iscariot, son of Simon, to betray Jesus. Jesus knew that the Father had put all things under his power, and that he had come from God and was returning to God; so he got up from the meal, took off his outer clothing, and wrapped a towel around his waist. After that, he poured water into a basin and began to wash his disciples' feet, drying them with the towel that was wrapped around him.

He came to Simon Peter, who said to him, "Lord, are you going to wash my feet?"

Jesus replied, "You do not realize now what I am doing, but later you will understand."

"No," said Peter, "you shall never wash my feet."

Jesus answered, "Unless I wash you, you have no part with me."

"Then, Lord," Simon Peter replied, "not just my feet but my hands and my head as well!"

Jesus answered, "A person who has had a bath needs only to wash his feet; his whole body is clean. And you are clean, though not every one of you." For he knew who was going to betray him, and that was why he said not every one was clean.

When he had finished washing their feet, he put on his clothes and returned to his place. "Do you understand what I have done for you?" he asked them.

"You call me 'Teacher' and 'Lord,' and rightly so, for that is what I am. Now that I, your Lord and Teacher, have washed your feet, you also should wash one another's feet. I have set you an example that you should do as I have done for you. I tell you the truth, no servant is greater than his master, nor is a messenger greater than the one who sent him. Now that you know these things, you will be blessed if you do them." ...

"A new command I give you: Love one another. As I have loved you, so you must love one another. By this all men will know that you are my disciples, if you love one another."

John 13:1-17, 34-35

TO SET THE SCENE

How well do you know each other? Write the answers to the questions you will be given on slips of paper. These will be put into bowls and some will be drawn out – can you identify who gave that answer?

Is our knowledge of these facts about each other a true measure of how deep friendships are within the group?

Read John 13:1-17, 34-35

1. What does the passage say that Jesus knew before he washed the disciples' feet (v1-5)? He was sure of his identity and calling and yet chose to serve. Have you seen other Christians do similar acts of service, or have you done them yourself?

HOW DOES THIS **2.** The church is to be a community of disciples, growing together in Jesus, marked by their love for each other. As such the church
APPLY TO ME needs to:

a) Be a place of reality and vulnerability rather than image or performance. Is your church a place where people feel free to express struggle and doubt? What about your housegroup? How can you encourage people to be more real about their faith?

> *'Pretending is the common cold of evangelicalism.'*
> **Gordon McDonald**

b) Be a pastoring community rather than a community with a pastor. What's the difference between the two? How can you be more effective in your pastoral care of one another?

c) Equip people for real life with relevant teaching. What subjects or areas of life would you like to have Christian teaching on, and in what context?

d) Be committed to the nurture of new Christians. Think back to when you made a commitment to follow Jesus. What or who was instrumental in helping that commitment to grow?

ENGAGING WITH

THE WORLD

3. Turn to Page 28 and think about how welcoming and inclusive other clubs or institutions are.

4. Look back at the learning experiences that Jesus provided for his disciples (Session 3, Question 3). Where do, or could, these experiences take place in your church community, especially for new Christians?

5. Jesus washed the disciples' feet, as a sign of his love and humility. What is an equivalent task that we could do for one another today?

HOW DOES THIS

APPLY TO ME

6. It is easy to analyse the church and talk about what needs to change. What action will you take, as individuals or as a group, as a result of this evening? Be positive and major on what you as individuals need to do, not what others have to do, particularly those who are not present!

> 'The task of the church is not to make men and women happy – it is to make them holy.'

> **Charles Colson**

WORSHIP

On a large sheet of paper draw an outline of your church building. Spend some time praying for the church. As you pray, paint the building and its surroundings, using colours to represent your prayers. Someone who wants to pray that the Bible becomes more foundational to the life of the church could paint a thick band of colour across the bottom of the building. Swirls of silver or white could represent the Spirit flowing through the church. Bright yellow around the church could accompany a prayer that the church is a light to those around it. The body of Christ is not confined to a building and painting around the building shape could represent this. Perhaps this picture could be put on a notice board at the church.

DURING THE WEEK

Put into action your decision in response to Question 6.

FOR FURTHER STUDY

Find out more about initiatives aimed at helping Christians in the workplace. A good place to start is The London Institute of Contemporary Christianity website: http://www.licc.org.uk/

Or visit the Spring Harvest site to find out the latest on their At Work Together conferences: http://www.springharvest.org.uk/awt/

ACTIVITY PAGE

Identify a couple of other clubs, communities or institutions you are part of – perhaps work, parents-at-the-school-gate, a sports club, evening class or discussion group. Think back especially to how you felt when you joined them. Write their names at the top of the first two blank columns, with a third column for your church and give each of them marks out of 10 for the areas below.

	Club 1	Club 2	Church
How welcome did you feel?			
How quickly did you feel you belonged?			
How easy was it to understand the 'rules' of the club – how you were to behave?			
Can anyone join?			
Were you able to participate?			
Were you able to help shape the club?			

What is the downside of comparing the church with other clubs in this way? Is there anything you can learn from these other places, and apply to your church?

REAL WAYS TO REACH OUT

AIM: To learn about incarnational evangelism from the example of Jesus

Incarnational evangelism: Jesus totally identified with us and yet remained the son of God. We need to identify with those around us without losing our identity as the people of God.

> *"I am coming to you now, but I say these things while I am still in the world, so that they may have the full measure of my joy within them. I have given them your word and the world has hated them, for they are not of the world any more than I am of the world. My prayer is not that you take them out of the world but that you protect them from the evil one. They are not of the world, even as I am not of it. Sanctify them by the truth; your word is truth. As you sent me into the world, I have sent them into the world. For them I sanctify myself, that they too may be truly sanctified.*

> *"My prayer is not for them alone. I pray also for those who will believe in me through their message, that all of them may be one, Father, just as you are in me and I am in you. May they also be in us so that the world may believe that you have sent me. I have given them the glory that you gave me, that they may be one as we are one: I in them and you in me. May they be brought to complete unity to let the world know that you sent me and have loved them even as you have loved me.*

> *"Father, I want those you have given me to be with me where I am, and to see my glory, the glory you have given me because you loved me before the creation of the world.*

> *"Righteous Father, though the world does not know you, I know you, and they know that you have sent me. I have made you known to them, and will continue to make you known in order that the love you have for me may be in them and that I myself may be in them."*

John 17:13–26

TO SET THE SCENE

What evangelistic activities or missions have you been involved in? How did you feel about them, then and now? Did they result in new disciples of Christ?

ENGAGING WITH THE WORLD

1. Words that are sometimes used to describe the culture we now live in are post-Christian, postmodern, multicultural or multifaith. Has it become more difficult to share the good news of Jesus?

> 'There was a part of me that secretly felt that evangelism was something you shouldn't do to your dog, let alone a friend.'
>
> **Rebecca Manley Pippert, Out of the Saltshaker, IVP**

2. These 'evangelistic' signs were displayed outside churches in the States one summer.

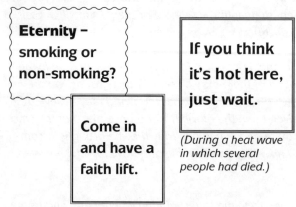

Eternity – smoking or non-smoking?

If you think it's hot here, just wait.

Come in and have a faith lift.

(During a heat wave in which several people had died.)

Are these accurate representations of the message of Jesus?

3. What is our message – what do we want to communicate about Jesus?

Read John 17:13–26

HOW DOES THIS

APPLY TO ME

4. Jesus said, 'As you sent me into the world, I have sent them into the world.'

How did the Father send Jesus? What are the implications for us as we engage in mission?

5. How do you balance being 'not of this world' (v16) with Jesus' model of incarnational evangelism?

6. Jesus said that the world would know that we are his disciples by our love for each other. How can we stop church communities appearing 'cliquey', like an exclusive club?

HOW DOES THIS

APPLY TO ME

7. Would you be accused of being 'a friend of sinners'?

ENGAGING WITH

THE WORLD

8. Look at the examples on the Activity Page of people finding ways of communicating the good news of Jesus to their communities.

HOW DOES THIS

APPLY TO ME

9. How can your housegroup be involved in incarnational evangelism? Meeting you could be the only opportunity many people have to meet Jesus, and to see the difference that knowing him makes. List the places where you meet and interact with people who are not Christians. What do they know about your faith, through what you say and what you do?

We are all involved in communicating the love of Jesus by the way we live our lives – we should ask ourselves how we can do it more effectively. Talk about the friends that people want to introduce to Jesus. How can the housegroup support them, and are there activities you can do together to this end?

ACTIVITY PAGE

INCARNATIONAL EVANGELISM DISCUSS THESE EXAMPLES:
A church in West Sussex cancelled their Sunday meeting in order to plant flower bulbs around the city at the request of the local council. They did so in an endeavour to be good news to their community, seeing that as more important than holding a service that morning. What do you think of their decision?

Christian youth workers on an estate in Hull started cleaning up the litter in their street each week. Young people came and asked them why they were doing it, and why there weren't any litterbins to put rubbish in. A few letters to the council later, litterbins were installed and the young people had a greater sense of ownership in their neighbourhood, as well as new friends in the youth workers. Is this evangelism?

Jim is a respected lay leader at his Anglican church and has served many years on the PCC. This autumn he decides that he will step down from the PCC in order to become a governor at the local school. Is he neglecting his gift of leadership? Or does that depend on what he achieves at the school?

A youth organisation in East Anglia runs a chaplaincy at a local nightclub. Some of their workers are there several times a week, to talk to clubbers, clean up people who are a bit worse for wear and take people home if they need it. Is this the kind of thing that Jesus would do?

Can you see ways in which you can get more involved in your local community?

WORSHIP
Choose something that represents the different issues you have covered each week. Put these on a table in the centre of the group. One or two people could talk about what made the biggest impression on them about each issue.

Spend some time in prayer, about the things that you have learned and the things you would like to do as a result.

DURING THE WEEK
After week 2, you were asked to think about whether you wanted to invite anyone round for a meal – perhaps now is the time to act on that if you haven't already.

FOR FURTHER STUDY
Look at how Paul addressed the people of Athens in Acts 17:16–34. He was speaking to people who didn't know about God, and who liked to discuss ideas. Contrast his approach with that of Peter in Acts 2, who was speaking to God-fearing Jews who were expecting the Messiah. Look at the different responses that they received: Paul in Acts 17:32–34; Peter in Acts 2:41. Why the difference? Would Paul have got a better response if he had just preached a straight 'gospel message'?

LEADERS' GUIDE

TO HELP YOU LEAD

You may have led a housegroup many times before or this may be your first time. Here is some advice on how to lead these studies:

▶ As a group leader, you don't have to be an expert or a lecturer. You are there to facilitate the learning of the group members – helping them to discover for themselves the wisdom in God's word. You should not be doing most of the talking or dishing out the answers, whatever the group expects of you!

▶ You do need to be aware of the group's dynamics, however. People can be quite quick to label themselves and each other in a group situation. One person might be seen as the expert, another the moaner who always has something to complain about. One person may be labelled as quiet and not be expected to contribute; another person may always jump in with something to say. Be aware of the different types of individuals in the group, but don't allow the labels to stick. You may need to encourage those who find it hard to get a word in, and quieten down those who always have something to say. Talk to members between sessions to find out how they feel about the group.

▶ The sessions are planned to try to engage every member in actively learning. Of course you cannot force anyone to take part if they don't want to, but it won't be too easy to be a spectator. Activities that ask everyone to write down something, or to talk in twos and then report back to the group, are there for a reason. They give everyone space to think and form their opinion, even if not everyone voices it out loud.

▶ Do adapt the sessions for your group as you feel is appropriate. Some groups may know each other very well and will be prepared to talk at a deep level. New groups may take a bit of time to get to know each other before making themselves vulnerable, but encourage members to share their lives with each other.

▶ Encourage a number of replies to each question. The study is not about finding a single right answer, but about sharing experiences and thoughts in order to find out how to apply the Bible to people's lives. When brainstorming, don't be too quick to evaluate the contributions. Write everything down and then have a look to see which suggestions are worth keeping.

▶ Similarly encourage everyone to ask questions, to voice doubts and to discuss difficulties. Some parts of the Bible are hard to understand. Sometimes the Christian faith throws up paradoxes. Painful things happen to us that make it difficult to see what God is doing. A housegroup should be a safe place to express all this. If discussion doesn't resolve the issue, send everyone away to pray about it, and ask your minister for advice!

▶ Give yourself time in the week to read through the Bible passage and the questions. Read the Leaders' notes for the session, as different ways of presenting the questions are sometimes suggested. However, during the session, don't be too quick to come in with the answer – sometimes we need space to think.

▶ Delegate as much as you like! The easiest activities to delegate are reading the text and the worship suggestions, but there are other ways to involve the group members. Giving people responsibility can help them own the session much more.

▶ Pray for group members by name, that God would meet with them during the week. Pray for the group session that it will be a constructive and helpful time. Ask the Lord to equip you as you lead the group.

THE STRUCTURE OF EACH SESSION

Feedback: find out what people remember from the previous session and if they have been able to act during the week on what was discussed last time.

To set the scene: an activity or a question to get everyone thinking about the subject to be studied.

Bible reading: it's important actually to read the passage you are studying during the session. Ask someone to prepare this in advance or go around the group reading a verse or two each. But don't assume everyone will be happy to read out loud.

Questions and activities: adapt these as appropriate to your group. Some groups may enjoy a more activity-based approach, some may prefer just to discuss the questions. Try out some new things!

Worship: suggestions for creative worship and prayer are included, which give everyone an opportunity to resopnd to God, largely individually. Use these alongside singing or other group expressions of worship. Add in a prayer time with opportunities to pray for group members and their families and friends.

For next week: this gives a specific task to do during the week, helping people to continue to think about or apply what they have learned.

For further study: suggestions are given for those people who want to study the themes further. These could be included in the housegroup if you feel it is appropriate and if there is time.

WHAT YOU NEED

A list of materials that are needed is printed at the start of each session in the Leaders' Guide. In addition you will probably need:

Bibles: the main Bible passage is printed in the book so that all the members can work from the same version. It will be useful to have other Bibles available, or to ask everyone to bring their own, so that other passages can be referred to.

Paper and pens: for people who need more space than is in the book!

Flip chart: it is helpful to write down people's comments during a brainstorming session, so that none of the suggestions is lost. There may not be space for a proper flip chart in the average lounge, and having one may make it feel too much like a business meeting or lecture. Try getting someone to write on a big sheet of paper on the floor or coffee table, and then stick this up on the wall with blu-tack.

GROUND RULES

How do people know what is expected of them during your meetings? Is it ever discussed, or do they just pick up clues from each other? You may find it helpful to discuss some ground rules for the housegroup at the start of this course, even if your group has been going a long time. This also gives you an opportunity to talk about how you, as the leader, see the group. Ask everyone to think about what they want to get out of the course. How do they want the group to work? What values do they want to be part of the group's experience: honesty, respect, confidentiality?

How do they want their contributions to be treated? You could ask everyone to write down three ground rules on slips of paper and put them in a bowl. Pass the bowl around the group. Each person takes out a rule and reads it, and someone collates the list. Discuss the ground rules that have been suggested and come up with a top five. This method enables everyone to contribute fairly anonymously. Alternatively, if your group are all quite vocal, have a straight discussion about it!

ICONS

The aim of the session

Engaging with the world

Investigate what else the Bible says

How does this apply to me?

What about my church?

NB not all questions in each session are covered, some are self-explanatory

SESSION 1

LEARNING FROM THE HUMANITY OF JESUS

MATERIALS NEEDED

Photos of group members when they were younger

The Miracle Maker video plus TV & video player, if using.

Magazines, labels, slips of paper, bowl (optional)

TO SET THE SCENE

You will need to contact people before the session and ask them to bring photos of themselves when they were younger. Give people time to talk about their photos – if you have a large group you may like to put people into twos or threes, otherwise it will take all night! This is a great way to get to know each other better, and makes the point that Jesus would have had memories too. We know very little about his first thirty years, but those years were important.

You could also show the first six and a half minutes of *The Miracle Maker*, the animation of Jesus' life. This clip gives glimpses of what Jesus might have done before he started his ministry, and ends with Mary sitting beside Jesus' bed with the gifts from the wise men.

1   Verse 1 is very clear – the Word was God. He gives the right to become children of God (v12). He came from the Father, full of grace and truth (v14).

2   People don't have to give exact chapter and verse of all their examples: but make sure they are from the Bible, not just their imagination. Here are some examples from John, but look at the other gospels too:

   Jesus was a wedding guest (2:2); a host (1:39); he travelled around (4:43); joined in festivals (2:23); ate dinner (12:2); was given an expensive and loving gift (12:3); served others (13:5); cooked breakfast (21:9). He experienced anger (2:16); thirst (4:7); persecution (5:16); rejection (6:66); grief (11:35); adulation (12:13); betrayal (13:30).

3   Emphasising his divinity can make Jesus seem aloof and distant, remote and powerful. It can be more difficult to appreciate his love for us. Highlighting his humanity can make him seem little more than a good teacher, a martyr perhaps. The events surrounding his birth can obscure the fact that he was a vulnerable baby. Christmas cards and carols present a sanitised picture: 'the little Lord Jesus no crying he makes' makes him seem otherworldly. The commandment not to make a graven image can make us wary of artistic representations of

Jesus and of imagining him as a real person. We are so used to having to defend and explain the fact that he was God, that we forget he was also human.

4   This is not to suggest that we should add to the Nicene Creed – after all it has served the church well since the fifth century. Statements could include Jesus' miracles, his friendships, his teaching, his lifestyle, his emotions and so on.

5   Respect the fact that people are making themselves vulnerable by sharing their difficulties.

6   Of course the two need not be mutually exclusive. However, singing songs in church on Sunday is less demanding than working out how to put Jesus at the centre of every part of our lives.

7   Jesus says 'apart from me you can do nothing', which implies that our efforts to be like him will not succeed unless he fills us with his Spirit and his life. But we can't just sit back and wait to be transformed. We need to cooperate with what Jesus is doing in our lives, setting our wills to serve him.

8   Write different areas of life on slips of paper and put them in a bowl: work, exercise, parenting, shopping, gardening and so on. Ask people to pull one out and discuss how to put Christ at the centre of that area of life.

9   Have magazines available for people to flick through, or ask one of the group to make a collage in advance depicting the lifestyle sold through adverts. People can write words on labels and stick them on the collage to show how life with Jesus at the centre is different.

WORSHIP
Play some music in the background as people say the creed to provide a worshipful atmosphere.

DURING THE WEEK
Remind people that you will be asking how they got on at the start of the next session.

SESSION 2

THE BANQUET – FOOD AND FRIENDSHIP

MATERIALS NEEDED
A three-course meal (see below)
Bread, wine and liturgy for communion, if using
Candle and nightlights (optional)

FEEDBACK
As people arrive, find out if they remembered to think about Jesus' humanity during the week. Was it helpful?

To prepare for the meal
The emphasis in having a meal together is to enjoy one another's company, to talk and share each other's lives and to deepen relationships. Calling it a banquet doesn't mean that you have to put on a huge, rich meal. Having three courses enables people to spend lots of time talking, but the food can be as simple or as elaborate as you like.

You may find it easier to ask a member of the housegroup to prepare the food, or ask everyone to bring contributions, so that you can direct people to do the readings and discuss the questions. You don't have to stick rigidly to the questions

– they are there as a helpful framework to conversation over the meal. Share the readings out amongst members of the housegroup. You may like to read out the paragraph at the end of last week's session at the start of the meal, reminding people why you are eating together. Then follow the suggestion in To Set the Scene, and pray.

Before the starter
1   It could be that only the disciples, Jesus' mother and the servants knew where this amazing new wine had come from. It resulted in the disciples putting their faith in Jesus.

2   The new wine of the kingdom of God contrasted with the old wine of the Jewish faith. John talks about this contrast in his prologue to the gospel (1:17).

3   Jesus brought the opportunity of relationship with him that would do away with the requirements of the law. We can be cleansed and forgiven through Jesus' death and resurrection, not by ritual washing that needs to be done repeatedly.

To discuss during the starter
4 If you think people are unlikely to know other stories from the gospels, put summaries of the following stories on slips of paper to be read out. Luke 5:27–32; Matthew 14:13–21; Luke 19:1–10; Luke 7:36–50; Luke 11:37, 14:1; Matthew 26:17–30; Matthew 11:19; John 21:9–14

5 As you discuss how our lives can become more banquet-like, make sure people stay on the themes of celebration, friendship and nourishment. It's not about becoming wealthy, important or exclusive!

To discuss as you eat the main course:
6 Bread, in different forms, is a staple food across the world, eaten every day by millions of people. It is not a food for special occasions; it is not only for the wealthy. It satisfies hunger and is good for us. Bread also symbolises that Jesus is available for everyone – he is the Saviour of the world (John 4:42).

7 Encourage the diversity of ways in which Jesus nourishes us to come out in conversation. The most obvious answers are through prayer, fellowship, preaching, and Bible reading. But Jesus can also nourish and sustain us through the beauty of creation, through sacrifice and service, through conversations with friends, and so on.

To discuss as you eat dessert
8 Followers of Christ are to be humble, not drawing attention to themselves, not full of their own importance. People can chose not to come to the banquet or to be part of the kingdom of God, but everyone is invited.

After the meal
WORSHIP
Denominations have different traditions surrounding communion. Some may only share bread and wine together if there is an ordained priest present, so adapt this section as appropriate to your church setting.

FOR FURTHER STUDY
You may feel that this is an essential thing to discuss during the meal, in which case substitute it for one of the other topics.

SESSION 3

BECOMING DISCIPLES OF CHRIST

MATERIALS NEEDED

Large sheet of paper, marker pens
Garden twine, leaves and paper if doing the collage option
Names on slips of paper and bowl
Bunches of grapes to look at and eat (optional).

FEEDBACK

Find out if anyone has planned to invite friends round. You could pray for these meals and friendships at an appropriate time during the evening.

TO SET THE SCENE

Refer back to these effective ways of learning as you discuss the opportunities that the church provides for learning.

1   Jesus firstly calms their fears at the thought of him leaving them by talking about the Holy Spirit. He tells them to expect the world's hatred, and reassures them of his love (chapters 15 and 16). Then he prays – for himself, for his disciples and for all believers. Jesus was preparing the disciples for life without him, and for the work that they would have to do. He wants them to be assured of his love and his continuing presence through the Spirit, to have a realistic under-standing of the difficulties ahead, but also to have a clear vision of their role in mission and how they will be equipped for it.

2   A disciple is literally a pupil or learner; an apprentice, one who spends time learning skills or a trade which they will then practise, and can pass on to others. A convert is someone who has made a decision for Christ; a disciple is someone who continues to learn about Jesus and is transformed in that process. Disci-pleship is not just for new Christians – we can all continue to learn from Jesus, throughout our lives.

3   John 2:11: they saw his miracles
    Matthew 5:1–12: they heard his teaching
    Matthew 10:1–15: they learned by doing
    Matthew 14:22–33: they were allowed to fail
    Matthew 18:1–6: they asked questions
    Matthew 26:36–46: Jesus needed their support
    Luke 9:18–21: they had to answer questions – to form an opinion
    We can't share these same experiences directly with Jesus today – who can we learn from?

4 Vines would have been pruned twice – once in the winter when all the old, dead branches were cut off, and once in the spring when extra branches that weren't likely to produce fruit were trimmed. This is why verse 2 refers to cutting and cleaning. Verse 3 implies that the word of God has a role in our pruning – giving us a standard against which to measure ourselves. Jesus also talks about the difficult times ahead for the disciples (15:18 onwards), which can be part of pruning (see Heb 12:7–11). In what other ways have people felt God pruning them – cutting back what does not give glory to him and helping them focus?

5 Jesus says that if we obey his commands we will remain in his love. Although this may seem to lean towards legalism or trying to earn God's love, we need to remember that our relationship with Jesus comes first. Out of that flows a desire to serve and please him – right behaviour.

6 Verse 8 – in order to glorify the Father. Not to be better people, or be more acceptable to God, or to feel good about ourselves, but to glorify the Father.

7 Being chosen by Jesus conveys a sense of privilege, of responsibility, and of permanence (John 10:27–30). We are very good at changing our minds – but we belong to Christ by his choice. That does not mean that we are forced to follow Jesus, but the initiative comes from Jesus, not us.

You could make this more of a collage, by providing garden twine and paper or real leaves for people to make their own section of vine. Encourage people to write on the leaves things they want to do in order to be a more committed disciple, or things they would like prayer for.

DURING THE WEEK

You can make sure each person is prayed for by putting names into a bowl and having each person draw one out. People can give specific prayer requests or just pray generally. This association between prayer and fruit may well remind people to keep praying beyond just one week!

FOR FURTHER STUDY

In this passage Jesus commands us to remain in him (v4), and to love each other (v12). Jesus said he didn't come to abolish the law but to fulfil it (Matt 5:17) and sums up the law as to love God with all your heart, soul, and mind and to love our neighbour as ourselves. Our righteousness is to surpass that of the Pharisees (Matt 5:20), which does not mean a greater legalism, but a deeper righteousness, following the spirit of the law, not the letter. For this we need to be transformed by Jesus.

SESSION 4
KNOWING GOD AND BEING KNOWN

MATERIALS NEEDED
A plant pot for each person
Compost and seeds – perhaps sunflower seeds
Parcel labels with string to attach to the pots; pens

FEEDBACK
Did people remember to pray for each other? Did anyone have a particularly 'fruity' week?

TO SET THE SCENE
Sometimes a crisis can help you appreciate friends more, or an extended time spent with someone, perhaps on holiday or a business trip.

1   Jesus is the way to the Father. Anyone who knows him, knows the Father; anyone who has seen him, has seen the Father. Jesus is returning to the Father to prepare a place for them and us. Jesus is in the Father and the Father is in him, a statement of their intimacy and that Jesus is truly divine. Jesus wants to bring glory to the Father.

2   You could write these verses out on slips of paper for people to read out. Or split the group into pairs and give each a few references to look up and report back on.

   John 5:19: the Son does what he sees the Father doing
   John 6:57: he was sent from the Father and lives because of him
   John 10:30: Jesus and the Father are one
   John 13:1: Jesus was to return to his Father
   John 14:6: no one comes to the Father except through Jesus
   John 14:21: those that love Jesus are loved by the Father.

3   More references to look up:
   Luke 6:12: he prayed, this time spending the night in prayer
   Luke 4:1,2: he fasted
   Luke 5:16: he spent time alone with God
   Luke 4:16: he went to the temple to worship.

   Can anyone think of other 'disciplines' that Jesus practised?

4 The aim of this session is not to make people guilty if they don't practise any disciplines, but to leave them intrigued and hungry to find out more. Give space if necessary for people to discuss the misuse of spiritual disciplines to get this out of the way. Spiritual disciplines can't earn us favour with God, or be a means of trying to manipulate God. Some disciplines can seem to legitimise a harmful form of self-denial. Don't allow the session to be hijacked with negativity – encourage people to be prepared to try something new.

5 Encourage a diversity of responses. Just as we all communicate differently with each other due, in part, to our different personalities, so some people will find some forms of prayer more helpful than others. Encourage honesty too.

6 Again, get people to share their experiences and what works for them. Some people have responded to a legalistic application of quiet times by not wanting anything more to do with them – but times of prayer and study can only benefit us. Listen to people's cries of how busy they feel. Time for prayer can feel like one more pressure – find ways to encourage people to make time because they want to, not because they ought to.

7 Mike Riddell has said that the closest any of us get to a desert experience is sitting on our own in a traffic jam. Whether or not you agree with that, silence and solitude are not easy to find in our busy lives – unless we learn to capture the moment, or make space.

8 Some people may be happy to cancel church if it was for a spiritual celebration – rather like another church service. Think of what there is to celebrate in your community or family life.

WORSHIP
You may want to do this outside, if it's the right time of year, or round the kitchen table as it can be a bit messy. Play music to provide a worshipful atmosphere and encourage people to pray as they plant their seed.

DURING THE WEEK
Do emphasise to people that a week-long trial is not an appropriate way to integrate a new discipline into one's life. This is more about identifying new spaces of time, or ways to draw close to God. It is easy to get into a routine and follow the same pattern each week – encourage them to try something new.

SESSION 5

CHURCH AND OUR RELATIONSHIPS

MATERIALS NEEDED

Slips of paper, pens and bowl
Large sheet of paper, paints and brushes

FEEDBACK

Ask how people got on with trying a new routine to their week in terms of prayer or another spiritual discipline. Be sensitive, so that people don't feel failures if they forgot, or were unable to make time. Encourage people to persevere.

TO SET THE SCENE

Think up about eight questions to ask the group such as: what do you do for work? What was your nickname as a child? Where did you go for a holiday last year? Provide lots of slips of paper. Ask the questions one by one. Each person writes their answer on a slip of paper and hands it in so that all the answers to question one are in a pile. Now comes the quiz. Hand everyone a sheet of paper to record their answers. Ask the questions again and read out a couple of answers to each from the appropriate pile of slips of paper. Group members should write down who they think gave that answer. You could argue that knowing these kinds of facts are not a true measure of friendship, but they could be an indication of how involved in each other's lives we are.

1   Jesus knew that it was time to leave the world and return to his Father. He knew that the Father had put all things under his power. He knew that he had come from God and was returning to God.

2   a) People can sometimes feel that they ought to know the answers, or should toe the party line in a church. Unbelief and unquestioned belief are enemies of the faith, but doubt should be valued as a spur to growth. b) Jesus discipled just twelve people at once, so is it fair for us to designate the pastoral care of hundreds of people to one person? People can be very hurt by a lack of pastoral care. Try to steer the discussion to how the church could be more pastoral, but perhaps follow up with people afterwards if anyone seems to have had particularly bad experiences in the past. c) Research has shown that few people hear sermons on the workplace, and yet that is where we spend most of our lives. Is this an area where people would like teaching, or are there others? Think too about how people would like to learn – sermons in church services are one vehicle, but are they the most effective? Make a note of any subjects for future housegroup courses!

3 You may find that the church doesn't do too badly compared with some other clubs. If people are too busy with church activities to be part of other clubs, discuss whether they want to do anything about that!

4 To remind you of what they are: The disciples: saw his miracles, heard his teaching, asked questions, had to answer questions – to form an opinion, learned by doing, were allowed to fail, Jesus needed their support, Jesus set an example. Think about how new Christians can be given these experiences in a church community.

6 You may feel it is appropriate to let the church leaders know how you feel as a group. Make sure that this is done with respect, and is accompanied with offers of help and commitment.

WORSHIP

Provide paints of different colours. If this is a new idea, give people a few ideas of what they could do.

SESSION 6

REAL WAYS TO REACH OUT

MATERIALS NEEDED
Something to represent each session
Flip chart and pens

TO SET THE SCENE
Discuss how members of the group came to faith – how many can identify a time or date when they became a Christian? Did it happen through meetings and missions, or relationships? What has kept them going since – why are they still Christians?

1   You don't need long analyses of what these words mean. You are looking for general feelings about how much our culture welcomes the good news about Jesus. Some would argue that an acceptance of many faiths gives space for us to share what we believe; others would say that there is more tolerance to every other faith than Christianity. Whatever the context we live in, do we see the need, and are we willing, to communicate our faith in Christ?

2   An emphasis on a choice between heaven and hell can miss out the need for discipleship, or any sense of what we are saved for. Salvation can be seen as an escape from this life, rather than the means to engage fully in the kingdom of God now as well as in the future. 'Come in and have a faith lift' makes it sound like faith is a superficial optional extra to make you more attractive, rather than an integral part of life.

3   Get a flip chart and brainstorm all the different things that people would want to communicate about Jesus. Learning 'four steps to salvation' or a specific illustration to explain the gospel can be useful, but there is a danger that we miss out as much as we say. Having a lot to communicate underlines the fact that evangelism is a process – it takes time to say all this, rather than covering it all in just one event or meeting.

4   Again, a flip chart might be useful here to list what people say, and then refer to it for the second part of the question. We have looked at Jesus' humanity, the image of a banquet as the life he calls us to and his relationships. The Father sent Jesus to 'live among us' – the incarnational approach. He shared our lives. He came to us, rather than expecting us to go and find him. He was confident of his calling and identity, not apologetic. Philippians 2:5–8 says that Jesus came to earth to serve, with humility. He made himself nothing.

Look at each of these answers and ask; 'What does this mean for me as I engage in mission?'

5 Some Christians have withdrawn from the world in response to verses like this – avoiding things like cinema, politics and theatre because they are worldly. Jesus engaged fully with life, and was accused of being a friend of sinners. We are not of this world because we are God's children and part of the kingdom of God. Jesus doesn't want us to withdraw from the world (v15), but recognises being his disciple can provoke a strong response.

6,7 Sometimes it seems difficult to get it right. If we don't spend enough time with other Christians, how can our love for each other show that we are Jesus' disciples? But if we spend too much, then we are neglecting those outside the church. Somehow Jesus managed to do both – but then that was his job, wasn't it?! As always, it's a question of balance. Listen to each other. Discuss how to discern imbalance and what you can do about it.

8 You could discuss what is good news for your community – planting bulbs may not be appropriate, so what could you offer?

FOR FURTHER STUDY
Paul started where his listeners were, with what they already accepted as true. He used examples from their culture and their world. Our message needs to match our audience. Peter spoke to people who were ready to hear what he was saying – the ripe harvest fields that Jesus had talked about.